SARAH PARDEE WINCHESTER
— A DRIVEN WOMAN —
HER COMPELLING STORY

Published by REDWOOD PUBLISHERS
240 Nice Lane, #308
Newport Beach, California 92663

Photographs Courtesy of Winchester Mystery House, San Jose, CA.

Cover Illustrated by Julie Grant

ISBN: 0917928-02-4   (pbk)

Library of Congress Catalog No. TX 2020 941

Second Printing 1988

Third Printing 1991

Fourth Printing 1994

WINCHESTER MYSTERY HOUSE

SARAH PARDEE WINCHESTER
— A DRIVEN WOMAN —
HER COMPELLING STORY

By GENEVIEVE WOELFL

REDWOOD PUBLISHERS / NEWPORT BEACH, CALIFORNIA

A WORD OF APPRECIATION
In Sincere Gratitude To
Mr. Keith Kittle—Managing-Director
Winchester Mystery House
And His Capable Staff
And To
Sean Patrick McGuire
Whose Co-operation brought forth
Mrs. Winchester's Story

SARAH PARDEE WINCHESTER
— A DRIVEN WOMAN —
HER COMPELLING STORY

In 1883 forty-four year old Sarah Winchester set out for California from New Haven, Connecticut.

The long train ride afforded ample opportunity to review her life in New England and the great sadness which engulfed her.

Her baby daughter, Annie Pardee Winchester, had preceded her husband in death leaving Sarah utterly alone regardless of the vast fortune left her by William Wirt Winchester. This gentleman was the only son of Oliver Fisher Winchester, the Arms magnate, who so recently endowed Yale University with his enormous financial gifts.

Rolling over the plains and through the mountains of beautiful America, once again she heard the words of the Boston *Psychic* flooding her mind in their unbelievable portent.

"Mrs. Winchester", she began, "You must travel to the West Coast and there build a beautiful home of the most costly materials in woods, crystals and metals. "And", the lady added, "construction on this building must never stop day or night".

"I do not understand you", Mrs. Winchester exclaimed literally sitting on the edge of her chair, "whatever do you mean?"

"I'm saying that as long as work goes on continuously in making additions onto your house, just so long will you, Mrs. Winchester, remain alive", she answered leaning closer to the heiress in her confidential manner.

"But my dear lady", Mrs. Winchester said, now sitting straight up in the high-backed chair and staring intently at the Psychic, "however could such a thing be? And why?", she gasped.

As if her counsel were not absurd enough this unqualified, untrained, would-be message giver ignorantly made answer: "Dear Mrs. Winchester, I'm given to tell you that you, alone, can make restitution and balance the ledger for the thousands of men killed by Winchester firearms in the Civil

MRS. WINCHESTER READY FOR A DRIVE IN HER LOVELY CARRIAGE AT THE CARRIAG
gardener behind a hedge. Sarah preferred no pictures.

ENTRANCE. This is the only photograph of this lady of mystery. It was snapped by an unseen

War and in skirmishes all over the Country, and even in Wars to come in the near future", she said frowning at the inner sight she saw and shaking her head from side to side.

Had this Psychic been a spiritual Medium she would have interpreted the correct meaning of what came through to her mind and never conveyed so alarming and disturbing a message to the 'sitter'. All could have been a different story if Sarah had consulted a second Medium for verification. But, spirit-messages and Psychic Phenomena were new to Sarah. Silently she listened.

Sarah Winchester froze under the heavy responsibility suddenly thrust upon her. She sat immovable, as if before a Judge, pondering the strange sentence received.

The bumping of wheels on the rails matched the thumping of Sarah's heart in anticipation of a new start in California.

Surely she never expected that her new home there and her life within it as a bright, misunderstood gentlewoman would one day stand as a monument to *Communication with the Spirit-World.* She could not know that groups of visitors from all over the world would wend their ways through the confusing maze of parlors, bedrooms, libraries, and the beautiful ballroom. How could she imagine that these vacationers would be lured by the fabulous colorful gardens of flower-studded beauty and rich greenery encircling unique tossing fountains and a huge museum unlike any, near or far, at the heart of a still unsolved mystery?

Sarah Winchester carried with her the inheritance from the Winchester Arms Company of New Haven plus an income of $1,000.00 a day.

In 1866 the Honorable Oliver Fisher Winchester reputedly produced the famous *Winchester rifle*, an improvement over the old Henry rifle of the Civil War. Although not the inventor, Winchester owned the patent. His son, William Wirt Winchester, capably assisted him in the steadily expanding business with its famous 'trade' name. *Winchester Arms* were bought by the United States Government and used in many uprisings, the Spanish-American War of 1898 and also in World War I, long after the Civil War.

In the security of her twenty million dollars Mrs. Winchester reached the spot in the small town of San Jose, California, which beckoned with possibilities for her coming project. On this 161 acre site of lush countryside along the road to Los Gatos stood a little 8 room farmhouse (nucleus of a 160 room mansion) where hammers would sound relentlessly building additions plus additions, then tearing them out, only to restructure again and again. Day and night neighbors would shudder at the constant din. No money would be spared to build, and build, and build the *Sarah Winchester House—strangest, oddest building of such tremendous size in the world.*

Of all the fabulous stories originating in California perhaps the most flabbergasting is the tale of the *Winchester Mystery House*, the saga of a *psychic misunderstanding, misdirection and gross mistake.*

The widow's professional plans and books on construction were filed in the library near her *seance-room*, where Sarah actually received *spirit-guidance*, she believed.

Throughout the wandering structure of 160 rooms, off and on during construction, Mrs. Winchester used a pattern of thirteen. Forty-seven fireplaces, forty staircases, doors leading nowhere, secret passageways, blind chimneys, trap doors and closet doors opening into nothing but wall space —all wrapped in enigmatic mystery to confound the visitor.

Worlds of money brought to this palace the finest lumber; delicate woods in mahogany, ebony, rosewood and other exotic kinds from distant lands. Stained art-glass windows set into tiny framework of real German silver leading or bronze paid tribute to Tiffanys on Fifth Avenue. Mother-of-pearl inlays and carefully designed mosaic tiles be-splendored the mantles throughout, as well as the washbowls in the guests' quarters.

Ornate décor dominated in the thirteen bathrooms. Some featured intricate faces wrought by Japanese artisans, bordering the dressing room tables. But none trimmed mirrors. Only two mirrors graced this mansion. These stood in Mrs. Winchester's private sleeping room and her bath.

Gold and silver chandeliers with twinkling crystal prisms enriched the royal ballroom made for dancing of a hundred couples. Here the beautiful mirror faced the wall as if it did not exist. Men came from New York to lay the flooring in this room without using nails, an almost unheard of board-

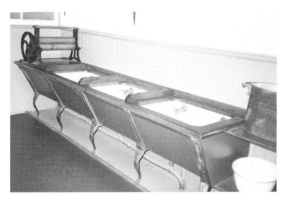

PORCELAIN LAUNDRY TUBS WITH MOLDED-IN SCRUB BOARDS AND SOAP DISHES were patented by Sarah Winchester. For this patent, she received $250,000.00 from the U.S. Patent Office.

A CENTER HALL AND STAIRWAY with many windows and detailed trim.

BLIND STAIRCASE LEADING TO THE CEILING in the WINCHESTER MYSTERY HOUSE. Beautiful workmanship, but it goes nowhere.

One of several kitchens. Here the hand carved soapstone sink with Daisy shaped drain shows 13 drain holes.

matching in that day. Two thousand dollars went into the front doors with special artwork of inlaid multicolored, gem-like triangles set by professional glassworkers—Tiffany's best.

The ballroom's imported stained glass windows displayed two quotations from 'Shakespeare' fashioned into the artwork:

WIDE UNCLASP THE TABLE OF THEIR THOUGHTS
THESE SAME THOUGHTS PEOPLE THIS LITTLE WORLD

Could it be that these words lent special meaning to the way of life for Sarah Winchester, guiding genius of this extraordinary enterprise for some thirty-eight years?

Sarah realized this exquisite ballroom needed live musicians with stringed instruments on the dais to lend to it the charm of culture, the grand *finis coróna ópus—the end crowns the work*. With the consent of her spirit-friends she offered $3,000.00 to *The Bostonians* to give a concert. At that time they were at the San Francisco Opera House. They regretted that previous commitments prevented acceptance of her invitation which they 'felt honored to receive". The Winchester glittering ballroom never enjoyed the brilliant entertainment for which it was built.

One wonders why, when this grand little lady ever sought the highest and best, she refused to open her front door to the President of the United States, Theodore Roosevelt, when he called in 1903. She could rightly be proud of this gorgeous place with its three elevators costing $10,000.00 each and Tiffany's exquisite Art-Glass windows in the entrance doors. The President preferred to miss seeing Mrs. Winchester rather than enter by the proffered Carriage-door.

Margaret Marriott, niece of Mrs. Winchester, her heiress, and Secretary, lived with her (her only companion). It was Margaret who made all necessary contacts with the outside world, and kept all curiosity seekers away from the mistress of the mansion. Mrs. Winchester would speak only with her building contractor and those servants with whom it was necessary to converse. She always wore a veil so no one could see her face. (Perhaps she thought her *spirit-friends* wished it so.) Sarah seemed especially attracted to the number thirteen. Stairways show 13 steps; ceilings, 13 panels;

chandeliers hold 13 lights; rooms with 13 windows, and many of these contain panes of specially cut glass.

Only one shower graced this elegant home. It was Sarah's personal thermostatically controlled water-spray geared to her 4 foot 10 inch height. Of course, it was located in the 13th bathroom featuring 13 windows.

The work for this vast project began with twenty-two laborers who strictly followed directions. Landscape gardeners used plans for making fences of tall hedges to conceal the entire property from the roadway while building went on. Seven Japanese gardeners served throughout the years keeping this wall of green in perfect condition.

Carpenters found it easy to execute the building work from Sarah's plans, which showed a master touch. Her study of technical books, magazines and engineering plans contributed to this; also, she was continuously receiving *spirit-guidance* in her *Seance-room*.

No one other than Sarah ever set foot in this sanctuary. Every day she sat there in *Meditation* until she received ideas for the work at hand. She would write them down on paper and then Margaret, her Secretary, would follow through on them.

None of the construction was "rush job", yet not a day passed without the swing of hammers, be it Sunday, a holiday or even Christmas. All the laborers wondered about this. Of course they could not know that a *Boston Psychic* assured Mrs. Winchester that the mischievous ones, poltergeists, would be kept out by good *spirit-people* as long as the owner endeavored to gratify them and *build*.

The Winchester House ended up with 160 rooms; however, during the construction carpenters pounded away completing numberless bedrooms, large and small, and ante-rooms, then ripped them all out. It must have been that conflict went on between Sarah's *spirit-friends*. Some wanted building one way and others another. Instead of being difficult, the *spirit-entities* may only have wished to help Sarah keep the hammers busy. They knew she must keep them ringing.

And perhaps Mrs. Winchester liked her spirit-helpers near her for company. Contrariwise, the mansion could easily have been equipped with every

THE GRAND BALLROOM with two exquisite leaded art glass windows showing two puzzling quotations from the Works of Shakespeare also boasts a parquet floor of six rare hardwoods put together with wooden pegs and glue. Here the chandeliers with 13 panels above hold 13 gas outlets. Sarah spent $9000.00 to make this room.

known arrangement, trap and idea for scaring away unwelcome spirits. By now a 'ghost-alarm' box could be residing in every room. Somehow Sarah got the notion that ghosts don't like mirrors around.

It's said they'll vanish immediately upon seeing their reflections in a mirror. It would be a simple matter for a builder to install a cheval glass swinging mirror on each side wall of every room. This would keep all *spirit-people* away, but surely this wasn't what Sarah wanted. She would do nothing to cause her *spirit-friends* to remain away. She depended upon their daily guidance. And she felt sure that the American Indian *spirit-guides were working with the carpenters as they built the steeples, turrets and towers. She felt good about their coming. In fact, in her own seance-room these Redmen-Spirits* told Sarah that they never blamed her for the deaths of so many of their tribesmen because she, herself never invented nor made the Winchester rifle, that famous 1873 "gun that won the West".

Once Sarah started her building program she trusted every word that came to her in her seance-room in meditation. What she received must have been *colored* by her own mental desires. All she thought about was 'building'. In fear she followed the false advice given her in Boston. She should have listened to someone better attuned to *spirit-communication* than she. Consequently, unlike other pretentious homes, Mrs. Winchester's featured no walls of resplendent mirrors to cast reflections. According to what little the widow knew of *ghosts*, these 'specters' enjoyed disappearing up chimneys. Sometimes they achieved entrance this way. Sarah tried to make things as easy as possible for her strange 'friends' that she knew to be with her spiritually.

For their convenience she built 47 fireplaces, so when it was time for them to go or come, there would be no congestion. She located one fireplace right out on her own personal sunporch for accommodation of 'spirits' who might need to leave quickly at the tolling of the great bell. Sarah's workmen built a tall bell tower. Inside this structure stood a wall so highly polished that it never could be scaled. The long bell drop fell straight to the cellar floor.

Only a trustworthy Japanese and his assistant knew the way through intricate underground passages to reach this place.

The Winchester bell pealed out at midnight, 1:00 am and at 2:00 am.

While planning this belfry, Sarah recalled from an old *ghost* book that these were important hours for 'spirits'. All other dials on the clock were passed by without a tinkle. She felt the accuracy of time important so she arranged that the bell-ringer check daily with the astronomical observatory to ascertain if the chronometers operated correctly. His costly watch proved a perfect timekeeper. He seldom made an adjustment.

Neighboring ranchers did not appreciate the ringing of the bell at such strange hours. They needed the announcement of day-light times, but at night they wanted to sleep, of course.

According to the little lady of this big house, she bought and arranged all the luxurious furnishings for the comfort and enjoyment of her nice *spirit-friends.* Someday she would join them in the *Spirit-World* and wanted to do everything here a cultured lady would do, so she would be in the right association later to be welcomed by these *spirit-people.* To accomplish this she spent millions. Only the most costly articles from all over the world she felt good enough for her Victorian mansion.

Mrs. Winchester located her *blue Seance-Room* where it would prove difficult for others to find. Only she knew which stairways to climb and which to descend in the winding maze leading to this sanctuary with its built-in cabinets and writing table, where she kept paper and pencil for *writing automatically* when the time was right. Sitting there in *Meditation* she noted all ideas and suggestions that came to her. Next to her chair she kept a 'Planchette-Board', similar to a 'Ouija-Board', with letters and numbers on it. While the hand rests upon a small table atop the board, this indicator moves around pointing to letters to form words which *spirit-entities* wish to say.

Most of the stairs to this special room measured but two inches high. Sarah was troubled with 'arthritis'. It seemed difficult for her to climb steps. Some said it was to confuse the *'spirits'* she did not wish to see. Be that as it may, this room was one *with a view;* not to the outdoor garden in its floral grandeur, but down to the main kitchen below. From here above Sarah could keep an eye on the servants. And more spywells were also located in other sections of this *'departmented'* structure. Two were on her special sunporch.

WINCHESTER MYSTERY HOUSE AS IT LOOKS TODAY. After the earthquake which toppled the

three top stories, Mrs. Winchester kept the height of her home at four stories.

Here the center of the floor boasted a plate glass skylight, protected by a railing. Mrs. Winchester checked on all kitchen activities personally.

From this porch the whole valley could be seen. One of the window frames held a pane of optical glass used as a lens, which magnified the wide expanse of the countryside like a telescope.

Although there were hundreds of stairs Sarah rode the three elevators when possible. One carried her up ten feet to her boudoir. One wonders that she never seemed to be lost in the labyrinth of passageways and fake rooms. Did she use a special map? Her *'spirit-advisors'* assured her that such confusing arrangements would disturb the *unfriendly* ones in spirit, *who blamed the one bearing the name of the famous firearms for their deaths*; these would surely be deterred in locating her and her seance-room. Evidently Sarah had implicit faith in her good *spirit-friends*. No ghosts walking England's famous castles held more reverence and respect.

There were balconies upon balconies with windows opening onto more balconies with openings to step through and again be standing on a balcony already visited after passing through one-way doors, through twists and turns until at last reaching a would-be clothes closet in one of the bedrooms. All puzzling and disconcerting, to say the least. The drawers at the bottom of this clothespress wall underneath gigantic shelves were make-believe, as was also one of two doors there. The other doorway actually led into Sarah's precious *Blue Seance-Room*, its sole exit a narrow door barely eighteen inches off the floor.

Mrs. Winchester felt confident that blocks and quick turns would obstruct those *unhappy ghosts* of malicious intent. She would elude them all. She always made it to her sanctuary, and somehow her treasured *spirit-friends* found the way to some inner, secret entrance made expressly for these special guests. (No doubt.)

In one oversized room with deep drawers and built-in chests with tremendous lockers and bins, expert cabinetmakers labored using smoothest and most beautifully polished woods. These storage facilities held fabulous collections of rare silks and satins; exquisite Belgium *pillow laces*, handmade *filet laces* from France and Italy; linens from Ireland, especially embroidered in China and the Philippines. This room also housed bolts and bolts of luxurious materials shipped from India, China and the far corners of the earth to the express order of the lovely mistress of Winchester House.

Until after Mrs. Winchester's death no one but its owner and her niece-companion knew what treasures lay hidden for over thirty years behind the heavily guarded entrance to this hidden vault. Great vans carried it all away.

$5,500,000.00 went into the building of her home to keep builders, gardeners and other artisans ceaselessly at work installing everything of quality, design and material—be it the fire prevention system with fire-proofed walls, steel wool filling all spaces behind panelings, the bracket sidelights in both floors and ceilings. There had to be plenty of light to please the good *spirit-friends*. Sarah felt sure about this. Gas jets all over operated by merely pressing a button; one piece porcelain laundry tubs, still unchipped today, featured molded-in washboards with soap trays. (Sarah received $250,000.00 for a patent on this idea.) She expressly inserted window frames with a crank handle arrangement, which came into popular use many years later, when casement windows arrived.

A Perman coal burning Boiler steam heated the vast spread of rooms augmenting the 47 fireplaces to keep the household warm.

To house the owner's many treasures, workers set six immense safes in concrete, one of which they placed in a wall in the Ballroom. This protected Sarah's $30,000.00 Gold service. At the same hour every night, two servants carried the precious pieces to the heavily veiled mistress to be counted as done before the evening dinner, then to be replaced in the safe. Only one servant was permitted to see Sarah's face (the Chinese butler serving at the table).

One day she went down a hallway without a veil. Two servants passed by. She realized they had seen her, and immediately dismissed them with a year's pay.

It's thought that Mrs. Winchester strongly resembled Queen Victoria. Sarah was only 4 feet 10 inches high. For some unknown reason she was averse to having her picture taken and to letting people see her. Of course, that was her prerogative. Some newspaper men tried to setup cameras all over the property at the moment Sarah was relaxing in her garden gather-

Sarah Winchester's favorite Daisy bedroom on which the tower fell during the earthquake of 1906 while she slept. Of extraordinary design is the art glass in the Daisy windows imported from Vienna, Austria. It was in this bedroom that Sarah passed away of a heart attack in 1922.

ing flowers. *She was without a veil!* When she saw these strangers, she rushed into a hothouse, the dehydrator, and nearly perished from suffocation. More guards were hired and even watchdogs brought in to detect the approach of unknown visitors. The barks of these trained animals would frighten anyone—a perpetual alarm operating night and day.

No one ever tried to rob the Winchester Home. Its very construction made it burglar proof. How could a stranger find an exit for a quick getaway or a doorway at night when this was impossible for anyone in the daylight without a map? It was no secret that safes waited there filled with rare and precious jewels and other valuables, yet no one ever attempted a break-in.

Sarah's ingenuity produced a mansion with 2000 doors and 10,000 windows. Its thirteen bathrooms adjoined the 40 bedrooms. All 47 fireplaces, each of individual design, were hand-carved from woods of many lands showing beautiful grains of mahogany, cherry, teak and oak; also pipestone and Italian marble.

Mrs. Winchester installed heating systems with some gas and electric heaters in out of the way spots and corners. Some believe this was to please her *spirit-friends*. Was this also the reason she purchased a luxury-yacht, but never put foot on it, the reason she bought several beautiful homes, but never even looked at them? It was so reported. She did enjoy riding in her 1917 Pierce-Arrow limousine as well as in her luxurious carriage, and often she visited her relatives in the expansive Atherton home she purchased for their comfort.

Sarah and her niece dined alone on the finest of foods. They enjoyed wine with dinner and a liqueur afterwards. One day Sarah, herself, went down to the wine cellar to make a personal selection. Screaming hysterically, she rushed upstairs. On a side wall a *black hand* (print) stared back at her. (A workman could have left it there while building the cellar.) Sarah took it as a psychic warning against all liquor. She did a thorough job of sealing up the wine house. She walled it in. It's yet to be found!

The anguish of Mrs. Winchester's fear of death came to light when she passed over to the spirit-side of life. A map had to be prepared of the winding maze of rooms and places for the removal of furnishings, which took two months time. Even with a map, movers continually got lost, not knowing which turn to take and ending up where they started. This was called "the move of the century".

Although of peculiar structural plan, the Winchester House was durably built. On the whole, it quite well withstood the 1906 earthquake, which destroyed much of beautiful San Francisco, 50 miles to the North. Three stories fell off the top of the house that early morning—the fifth, sixth and seventh. Thereafter, the mansion remained no higher than four stories.

Mrs. Winchester's bedroom and bath received the greatest damage where window panes fell inward and plaster fell from ceilings and walls. In 1906 on April 18, that frightful day, Sarah was in bed. It was a jammed door that held her prisoner in her own castle for hours. It took the servants a long time to locate their mistress; from her room she could not be heard calling for help, so her niece thought she must be sleeping in another section of the house. Sarah's terror can be understood. She ordered her quarters closed and sealed. But later on they were reopened for her enjoyment in the favorite part of her vast home.

Sarah was born in 1840. A sudden heart attack took her into the higher life of the *Spirit-World* in 1922 at the grand age of 82. Now beckoned her native homeland in Connecticut for a lasting place of peaceful quiet. At long last the hammers were silent. Surely they became the knell of her *spirit-flight*. Perhaps now she could hear the more beautiful sounds she missed over the years. And 'music-of-the-spheres' would welcome her to the world of her *spirit-friends* whose companionship she cherished for thirty-eight years in the home she built on *spirit-direction*.

Mrs. Winchester provided work for hundreds of people for over a quarter of a century and left a monument to her conviction of the *existence of the Spirit-World*, the *continuity of Life* and to *spirit-communication*.

We will never know how much happier this dear lady would have been had she not chosen to live unto herself alone. A greater good might have come from a wider use of the millions she spent with fear of death, a Sword of Damocles, ready to fall should she stop building Winchester House, Llanda Villa.

Sarah Winchester might now be remembered as a giant benefactress of the City of San Jose. She might have constructed a Civic-Center nestled in floral parkways or built an unequaled Library enriched in volumes on the life and customs of peoples around the world with their contributions to civilization featuring the history and progress of our own great America. But an incident in Boston, Massachusetts set the pattern of her life instead.

Here is an example of the necessity for checking the Mediums consulted and testing their messages. Sarah's common sense should have made her skeptical. She should have tried to verify the spirit-message by consulting other Mediums too.

Inwardly Mrs. Winchester must have known that one day she would join her loved ones and relatives in the Spirit-World. And she did have an extensive will drawn up. It is reported that her will of 13 segments (units) was duly signed by Sarah in its 13 signature places.

When she died, September 5, 1922, both her attorney—the Honorable Roy F. Leib and her personal Physician—Clyde Wayland, M.D., spoke glowingly of this aristocratic lady. They declared her very sane. And her employees said that she was not eccentric in any way. Yet, Mrs. Winchester was convinced that the Spirit-World was very *real*. Had she not communicated with her friends living in that higher rate of vibration?

And Mrs. Winchester must have been a brilliant person. She professionally managed her huge home with the services of 10 housekeepers, 13 carpenters, 8 gardeners and her personal coachman and car attendants.

According to Harold F. Williamson, Ph.D., instructor at North Western University, in his book, Winchester—"*The Gun That Won the West*" (c) 1952, the well known writer William Melich expressed some interesting thoughts about Mrs. Winchester in the February 1947 Holiday magazine. Mr. Melich said that Sarah's attorney considered her a shrewd business woman who made a tidy amount of money in California Real Estate to add to her $1,000.00 a day income from her shares of Winchester Repeating Arms Co. and her patents, as well. Melich ventured to say that perhaps the absurd building of her home was in reality Sarah's hobby to keep her busy. Her doctor prescribed finding something to occupy her mind and time in a new location when she was overcome by grief over the loss of her daughter, Annie Pardee Winchester. Sarah's little girl was born June 15, 1866, and a month later on July 24 she passed away due to Marasmus (not able to assimilate

WINCHESTER MYSTERY HOUSE GARDENS OF THE WORLD reflecting Sarah Winchester's hobby of importing plants from all over the World. This vintage photo shows the House and Gardens at the turn of the Century, 1900.

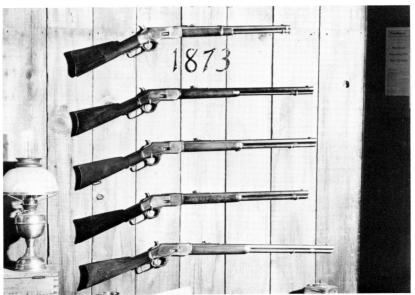

FAMOUS HISTORICAL RIFLES AT WINCHESTER MUSEUM including **THE FAMED WINCHESTER MODEL '73 – "THE GUN THAT WON THE WEST".**

food). This 'unbearable' shock was augmented in 1881 on March 7 when William Wirt Winchester, Sarah's husband, succumbed from Pulmonary Tuberculosis.

Sarah was the daughter of Leonard and Sarah Burns Pardee. As a beautiful young lady, Sarah was an accomplished musician and spoke four languages fluently. September 20, 1862 was her wedding day.

According to the *National Cyclopedia of American Biography*, several prestigious men of Pardee Lineage were descended from the same paternal American ancestor—George Pardee. He came from Pitminster, England (a native of Wales) during the Huguenot persecution circa 1683. Two years after arriving in this country he married Martha Miles and settled in New Haven, Connecticut. It was probably of an eighth generation later that Sarah Pardee married the son of Oliver Fisher Winchester in New Haven, Connecticut. No doubt Sarah's father could trace his ancestry directly to George Pardee.

Members of Oliver Winchester's family followed the precedent he set of donations where they would be of greatest benefit. To Yale University he donated a site on Prospect Street in New Haven for Yale Observatory in 1871 and the present Observatory site in 1879. In 1909, an added amount of $120,000.00 was given through endowment. In 1891, Jane Ellen Hope Winchester, wife of Oliver Winchester, gave $150,000.00 for Winchester Hall at Yale in memory of this President of Winchester Repeating Arms Co. She also established the William Wirt Winchester Fund with a gift of $15,000.00 in memory of her son, William Wirt Winchester, husband of Sarah, for the Yale Art School. Mrs. T.G. Bennett, sister of William Wirt Winchester added another $5,000.00 to this fund in 1899. In 1910, the Yale Medical School was established with an endowment by Mrs. Oliver Winchester which reached $150,000.00 by 1913.

Oliver F. Winchester was not a Yale graduate. In fact, his career was in the best American tradition. His successes were achieved by dint of hard work as a business tycoon.

At the early age of seven, he worked on a farm to help his widowed mother feed her family of 5 children. Oliver and a twin brother, Samuel, were only 1 year old when their father, a Boston farmer, died leaving nothing for his family. Oliver went to school in the wintertime and when he was in his teens, he learned carpentry and then the manufacturing of shirts and men's furnishings. He bought a store in Baltimore, Maryland. From this business, he accumulated a small fortune and was ready to buy 800 shares of Volcano Arms Co. taking it over and reorganizing it into the New Haven Repeating Arms Co. He became President and changed its name to Winchester Repeating Arms Co. of New Haven in 1866. He made his only son, William Wirt Winchester, the Vice-President at $3,500.00 per year. The Treasurer of the Board was William White Converse, who married Sarah's sister, Mary; he received $5,000.00 a year. Secretary of the Company was T.G. Bennett, who was married to one of Oliver's two daughters, Hanna Jane, with a salary of $3,500.00 per year. Tyler Henry, inventor of the Henry rifle from which the Winchester Repeating Rifle was later developed, was the Superintendent of the entire Plant.

In the beginning, Oliver Winchester knew nothing of the Arms manufacturing, but his ability lay in his skill in industry and salesmanship, and in his grasp of financial matters. He chose subordinates who could advise him on technical matters and decisions. This man learned by experience. His Company is now a Division of OLIN INDUSTRIES, INC.

In 1863, Oliver F. Winchester was Councilman of New Haven, Connecticut. He was Presidential Elector at Large for Lincoln. In 1866, he was Lieut. Governor with J.K. Hawley.

He was born in 1810 and had reached 70 years in 1880 when he passed on. Here was an amazing man starting with no capital, yet he left a Personal fortune of one and a half million dollars. After the death of the first President of Winchester Repeating Arms Company, from 1857-1880, his son, William Wirt Winchester, became the second in that office from 1880-1881 (until his early death). The third President was William Converse from 1881-1890. Thomas Gary Bennett then became the fourth President from 1890-1910 followed by George E. Hodson from 1911-1915. The sixth man for this Chair was Winchester Bennett from 1915-1918, followed by Thomas G. Bennett from 1918-1919, who was the seventh President of Winchester Repeating Arms Company.

In 1911, Mrs. Sarah Winchester established the William Wirt Memorial

Sanatorium for Tuberculosis endowing it with $1,200,000.00. This hospital opened in 1916 to help conquer the scourge of 'Galloping Consumption' raging throughout the entire Country. Sarah's philanthropies brought new hope to many of all faiths.

The residue of this lady's estate went to her niece, Margaret Merriman Marriot and to the General Hospital of New Haven, Connecticut.

Surely the angels, her spirit-friends, were not concerned with how much money was left. They would ask only: "What good things have you done, Sarah?" And that little lady could proudly answer:

"I built the WINCHESTER MYSTERY HOUSE
A Monument to the *Continuity of Life-After-Life*
And to *Communication with people in the Spirit-World.*"

In the now great metropolis of San Jose, third largest City in California with its burgeoning population approaching 600,000, stands the *Winchester Mystery House*, called *Llanda Villa* (Yawnda) by its Architect-Mistress-Builder, Sarah Winchester. To one researcher, she spiritually translated this Indian name to mean *Perfect One*.

Here at 525 South Winchester Boulevard, this famous mansion received the *California State Registered Historical Landmark No. 868* on May 13, 1974. On August 7, 1974, it was placed on the *National Register of Historic Places in Washington, D.C.*

It spreads over six acres between Interstate 280 and Stevens Creek Boulevard, fifty miles Southeast of San Francisco. It's easily accessible. This spectacular mansion of wandering connected rooms staggers the mind on approach in its setting of rich greenery and flowers with a drive bordered by 13 stately palms.

After Sarah went away, all furniture and accessories found new homes long before my first visit to this fascinating place in 1942. The building was empty except for a tiny entrance space selling postcards, candies and knick-

BEAUTIFUL LLANDA VILLA BEFORE THE 1906 EARTHQUAKE. WINCHESTER MYSTER
adjacent farmland in 1900. It had 90 rooms then; today it has 160.

HOUSE was built seven stories high. This unique jewel of Victorian architecture dominated the

knacks and offering flyers about Mrs. Winchester and her unusual home.

Gradually over the years and under the capable ownership-management, some of the Winchester original pieces drifted back and others of that 19th century returned to again dress up some twenty or more rooms.

And the spacious Gift Shop now features objects and articles from all over the world as well as beautiful mementos of the *Winchester Mystery House*. Enjoying this sparkling array displayed in all its splendor is an unforgettable privilege.

The restoration Board of Directors has committed itself to restoring the sprawling mansion to the same stately beauty it enjoyed when Mrs. Winchester, lady of mystery, wandered about her charming home. It's believed that this rejuvenation program will continue to permit Sarah P. Winchester, in her own way, to achieve a unique kind of eternal life. Rich furnishings of the Victorian and Edwardian periods make a familiar setting for the mistress of LLANDA VILLA—*Winchester Mystery House*.

Here the Winchester Historic Firearms Museum houses one of the largest collections of Winchester rifles and antique firearms on the West Coast including the 1860 Henry rifle, the first Winchester model 1866, also the famous 1873 "Gun That Won The West". It displays all kinds of such equipment with historical records of wars and war heroes. The Winchester Antiques Product Museum displays many old-time items and gadgets, iceboxes, skates, tools, lamps and a myriad of other articles made by the Winchester Company during this time period. They were marketed through some 6300 Country Stores all over America and through its mail order outlets.

This "walk through time" makes it easy to picture Mrs. Winchester, conferring with her builders; or to mentally see Oliver Winchester as he discusses an invention with his employee, B. Tyler Henry, whose patents helped the company attain its spectacular success; one might almost hear the barker's voice at Buffalo Bill's Wild West Show: "Foes in '76 and Friends in '85, when *Sitting Bull* agreed to join the Show because he wanted to see Annie Oakley shoot every day". And one might imagine T.G. Bennett, the Company's Secretary, and gunmaker, John Browning, planning new work. We must also witness the wild bunch of 1906, the daring robbers of the

Winnemucca Nevada Bank plotting with the leader, the notorious 'Butch Cassady' and the 'Sundance Kid' as they come to life in this historical 'journey'. They too, used a trusty Winchester.

Winchester Repeating Arms Co. was a worthy contributor to many important moments of frontier America including the ever amazing *House of Winchester*. Here precious letters to her attorney and banker arranging business matters, in Sarah's own handwriting, are protected under glass for all to see and examine.

30,000 new shrubs, trees, flowers and artistic fountains further enrich the grounds of the mansion adding to the spectacular glory of the 100 year rose bushes and 'feather and fan' Date Palms, rare Peruvian Pepper trees, European Black Forest Locust trees, English Walnut, Spanish Pine, Catalpus trees, Monkey-puzzle trees, Pink Crepe Myrtle, Persimmons, Orange, Lemon and Bayleaf, Pink Hawthorne, Star-Jasmine and Sarah's favorite, the Daisy.

Mrs. Winchester's gardenhouse with its thirteen cupolas is becoming active again in its vital spot of beauty. Other outside buildings are now restored and included on the Grounds Tour: the tank house, pump house, plumbers' workshop, garages, car wash and gardeners' tool shop. And from the old woodshed in the rear have emerged modern catering facilities for groups, clubs and conventions.

Because international interest draws visitors from the entire United States and many foreign countries, abridged tour brochures are now available in English, French, German, Japanese and Spanish.

The Estate Tour includes the 1 hour guided tour of the mansion's interior, a self-guided tour of the restored Victorian Gardens and outlying buildings, plus admission to both the Winchester Historic Firearms Museum and the Antique Products Museum. Guided tours are given every day of the year from 9 am except Christmas Day.

The Gift Shop and Sarah's Kitchen (Coffee Shop) are open daily. The Winchester Mystery House is located at 525 South Winchester Boulevard, San Jose, California 95128.

The Author, GENEVIEVE WOELFL AT SARAH WIN-CHESTER'S CARVED VICTORIAN TEA TABLE IN THE RESTORED FRONT PARLOR OF WINCHESTER MYSTERY HOUSE.

ABOUT THE AUTHOR

Genevieve Woelfl received her early education at Syracuse. Further studies in Comparative Religions, Metaphysics and in Scientific Research followed.

She graduated with honors from the Bureau of Education of the National Spiritualist Association with Teacher's Degree (N.S.T.).

She is an Ordained Minister of the Religion of Spiritualism. She is a Spirit-Writing Medium and Spiritual Counselor. She has lectured on Philosophy and Parapsychology in Colleges, libraries and Churches, where she has taught a Technique for successful Meditation.

WRITINGS by Genevieve Woelfl

PSYCHIC EXPERIENCE—*An Introduction to Spiritualism*
REDWOOD PUBLISHERS   1976

YOUR PSYCHIC SELF—*How-To-Use-It*

SARAH PARDEE WINCHESTER—A DRIVEN WOMAN—*Winchester Mystery House*
REDWOOD PUBLISHERS 1986